The HEART *of* LEADERSHIP

500 Timeless Quotes That Define Great Leadership

LOLLY DASKAL

Kevin,
Here's to the footprints
you'll leave behind.
Bobbi & Marquele

Printed in the United States of America

Lead From Within Publishing

ISBN-13: 978-0-692-78374-0
ISBN-10: 0-692-78374-1

Book design by Carrie Ralston, Simple Girl Design LLC

To Michaele, Ariel, and Zoe

My three beloved children, who have taught me over and over again what it means to lead from the heart.

Lead From Within Publishing
New York, New York

INTRODUCTION

What is leadership?

There are as many definitions of leadership as there are leaders. If you do an Internet search on the word *leadership*, you can get about 479,000,000 results, each definition as unique as an individual leader.

Leadership is a difficult concept to define, perhaps because it means so many things to different people.

This book has taken on the task of getting to the heart of what leadership is and how to define it. It has taken inspiration from those who have been our leaders in the past and from the most successful people who lead us today.

Pay attention to what you're about to read. Think about the words you see and the messages they convey.

More importantly, focus on how you can apply those messages in order to improve your life and the lives of others.

Here are 500 ways to get to the heart of leadership — choose the ones that fit you best and inspire you to lead from the heart.

DON'T BE AFRAID OF
BEING DIFFERENT.
BE AFRAID OF
BEING LIKE EVERYONE ELSE.

Lolly Daskal

Everyone is a leader to someone.
Whether that someone be an employee
(or thousands of employees), your spouse, a child,
or at the simplest level, oneself; you are a leader.

Tracy Brinkmann

The most dangerous leadership myth is that leaders
are born — that there is a genetic factor to leadership.
This myth asserts that people simply either have certain
charismatic qualities or not. That's nonsense; in fact,
the opposite is true. Leaders are made rather than born.

Warren G. Bennis

A leader takes people where they want to go.
A great leader takes people where they don't
necessarily want to go, but ought to be.

Rosalynn Carter

A leader is best when people barely know he exists...
when his work is done, his aims fulfilled,
they will all say: We did it ourselves.

Lao Tzu

Leadership should be born out of the understanding of
the needs of those who would be affected by it.

Marian Anderson

A good leader takes a little more than his share of the
blame, a little less than his share of the credit.

Arnold H. Glasow

The ultimate measure of a man is not where he stands
in moments of comfort and convenience, but where
he stands at times of challenge and controversy.

Martin Luther King Jr.

You don't need a title to be a leader.

Mark Sanborn

It is better to lead from behind and to put others
in front, especially when you celebrate victory when nice
things occur. You take the front line when there is
danger. Then people will appreciate your leadership.

Nelson Mandela

Successful leaders lead with the heart, not just the head.
They possess qualities like empathy,
compassion and courage.

Bill George

Leadership is the capacity and will to rally men
and women to a common purpose and
the character which inspires confidence.

Bernard Montgomery

I know of no single formula for success. But over the years I have observed that some attributes of leadership are universal and are often about finding ways of encouraging people to combine their efforts, their talents, their insights, their enthusiasm, and their inspiration to work together.

Queen Elizabeth II

Leaders must be self-reliant individuals with great tenacity and stamina.

Thomas E. Cronin

The task of leadership is not to put greatness into people but to elicit it, for the greatness is there already.

John Buchan

A great person attracts great people
and knows how to hold them together.

Johann Wolfgang von Goethe

When the leadership is right and the time is right,
the people can always be counted upon
to follow — to the end at all costs.

Harold J. Seymour

All of the great leaders have had one characteristic
in common: it was the willingness to confront
unequivocally the major anxiety of their people
in their time. This, and not much else,
is the essence of leadership.

John Kenneth Galbraith

THE GREATEST LEADER
IS NOT NECESSARILY THE ONE
WHO DOES THE GREATEST
THINGS. HE IS THE ONE THAT
GETS THE PEOPLE TO DO
THE GREATEST THINGS.

Ronald Reagan

The question isn't who is going to let me;
it's who is going to stop me.

Ayn Rand

The most basic of all human needs is the need
to understand and be understood.
The best way to understand people is to listen to them.

Ralph Nichols

It is the responsibility of leadership to provide
opportunity, and the responsibility of individuals
to contribute.

C. William Pollard

The roots of effective leadership lie in simple things, one of which is listening. Listening to someone demonstrates respect; it shows that you value their ideas and are willing to hear them.

John Baldoni

The art of communication is the language of leadership.

James Humes

One measure of leadership is the caliber of people who choose to follow you.

Dennis Peer

Real leadership is leaders recognizing that they serve the people that they lead.

Pete Hoekstra

Leadership is the capacity to translate vision into reality.

Warren Bennis

Leadership defines what the future should look like,
aligns people with that vision, and inspires them
to make it happen, despite the obstacles.

John Kotter

I start with the premise that the function of leadership
is to produce more leaders, not more followers.

Ralph Nader

Leadership is the capacity to influence others through
inspiration motivated by passion, generated by vision,
produced by a conviction, ignited by a purpose.

Myles Munroe

I think leadership comes from integrity — that you do whatever you ask others to do. I think there are nonobvious ways to lead. Just by providing a good example as a parent, a friend, a neighbor makes it possible for other people to see better ways to do things. Leadership does not need to be a dramatic, fist in the air and trumpets blaring, activity.

Scott Berkun

Leadership is unlocking people's potential to become better.

Bill Bradley

Leadership and learning are indispensable to each other.

John F. Kennedy

Leadership is the special quality which enables people to stand up and pull the rest of us over the horizon.

James L. Fisher

Effective leadership is not about making speeches or being liked; leadership is defined by results not attributes.

Peter F. Drucker

Innovation distinguishes between a leader and a follower.

Steve Jobs

Leadership is the art of getting someone else to do something you want done because he wants to do it.

Dwight Eisenhower

Leadership is simply causing other people to do what the leaders want. Good leadership, whether formal or informal, is helping other people rise to their full potential while accomplishing the mission and goals of the organization. All members of an organization who are responsible for the work of others have the potential to be good leaders if properly developed.

Bob Mason

The very essence of leadership is that you have to have a vision. It's got to be a vision you articulate clearly and forcefully on every occasion. You can't blow an uncertain trumpet.

Theodore Hesburgh

Leadership is the art of mobilizing others to want to struggle for shared aspirations.

James Kouzes and Barry Posner

IF YOUR ACTIONS
INSPIRE OTHERS
TO DREAM MORE,
LEARN MORE,
DO MORE
AND BECOME MORE,
YOU ARE A LEADER.

John Quincy Adams

Leadership is not a person or a position. It is
a complex moral relationship between people,
based on trust, obligation, commitment, emotion,
and a shared vision of the good.

Joanne Ciulla

The challenge of leadership is to be strong,
but not rude; be kind, but not weak; be bold, but not
bully; be thoughtful, but not lazy; be humble, but not
timid; be proud, but not arrogant; have humor,
but without folly.

Jim Rohn

Leadership is lifting a person's vision to high sights,
the raising of a person's performance to a higher
standard, the building of a personality beyond its
normal limitations.

Peter Drucker

Leadership is an opportunity to serve.
It is not a trumpet call to self-importance.

J. Donald Walters

Leadership is a matter of having people look at you
and gain confidence, seeing how you react.
If you're in control, they're in control.

Tom Landry

A leader is one who knows the way, goes the way,
and shows the way.

John Maxwell

Leadership is the process of persuasion or example
by which an individual (or leadership team) induces a
group to pursue objectives held by the leader or shared
by the leader and his or her followers.

John W. Gardner

A leader is a dealer in hope.

Napoleon Bonaparte

The highest calling of leadership is to
unlock the potential of others.

Lolly Daskal

Leadership is the ability to guide others without force
into a direction or decision that leaves them still feeling
empowered and accomplished.

Lisa Cash Hanson

The task of the leader is to get his people from
where they are to where they have not been.

Henry Kissinger

Leadership is about service to others and a commitment to developing more servants as leaders. It involves co-creation of a commitment to a mission.

Robert Greenleaf

Leadership is working with and through others to achieve objectives.

Paul Hersey

Management is about arranging and telling. Leadership is about nurturing and enhancing.

Tom Peters

Leadership is a potent combination of strategy and character. But if you must be without one, be without the strategy.

Norman Schwarzkopf

A GOOD LEADER LEADS THE
PEOPLE FROM ABOVE THEM.

A GREAT LEADER LEADS THE
PEOPLE FROM WITHIN THEM.

M.D. Arnold

A leader's role is to raise people's aspirations
for what they can become and to release their energies
so they will try to get there.

David R. Gergen

Effective leadership is putting first things first.
Effective management is discipline, carrying it out.

Stephen Covey

It's not where you are today that counts.
It's where you are headed.

Arthur F. Lenehan

It is better to ask some of the questions
than know all the answers.

James Thurber

It is better to choose what you say
than say what you choose.

Anonymous

It is much easier to be critical than correct.

Benjamin Disraeli

It is often our own imperfection which makes us reprove
the imperfection of others — a sharp-sighted love
of our own which cannot pardon the self-love of others.

François Fénelon

The price of greatness is responsibility.

Winston Churchill

The chief executive who knows his strengths and
weaknesses as a leader is likely to be far more effective
than the one who remains blind to them. He also is on
the road to humility — that priceless attitude
of openness to life that can help a manager absorb
mistakes, failures, or personal shortcomings.

John Adair

Thoroughness characterizes all successful men.
Genius is the art of taking infinite pains. All great
achievement has been characterized by extreme care,
infinite painstaking, even to the minutest detail.

Elbert Hubbard

Leadership is the key to 99 percent
of all successful efforts.

Erskine Bowles

Leadership is a matter of how to be, not how to do it.

Frances Hesselbein

Leadership is the ability to establish standards
and manage a creative climate where people are
self-motivated toward the mastery of long-term
constructive goals, in a participatory environment
of mutual respect, compatible with personal values.

Mike Vance

Leadership is getting people to work for you
when they are not obligated.

Fred Smith

One of the tests of leadership is the ability to recognize
a problem before it becomes an emergency.

Arnold Glasow

Leadership is the art of influencing others
to their maximum performance to accomplish
any task, objective or project.

W.A. Cohen

A good leader is a caring leader — he not only cares
about his people, he actively takes care of them.

Harald Anderson

There are almost as many definitions of leadership
as there are persons who have attempted
to define the concept.

Ralph Stogdill

The growth and development of people
is the highest calling of leadership.

Harvey S. Firestone

Keep your fears to yourself,
but share your inspiration with others.

Robert Louis Stevenson

Without passion, a person will have
very little influence as a leader.

Michele Payn-Knoper

Leadership is the process of turning followers into leaders.

Lolly Daskal

A leader is someone who demonstrates what's possible.

Mark Yarnell

LEADERSHIP IS DOING WHAT
IS RIGHT WHEN NO ONE
IS WATCHING.

George Van Valkenburg

Leadership is practiced not so much in words
as in attitude and in actions.

Harold Geneen

Never tell people how to do things. Tell them what to do
and they will surprise you with their ingenuity.

George S. Patton

Leadership by example is the only kind of real
leadership. Everything else is dictatorship.

Albert Emerson Unaterra

The leader is one who mobilizes others toward
a goal shared by leader and followers...
Leaders, followers and goals make up the three
equally necessary supports for leadership.

Garry Wills

The leader must know, must know that he knows,
and must be able to make it abundantly clear
to those around him that he knows.

Clarence Randall

Leadership is about taking responsibility,
not making excuses.

Mitt Romney

Great leadership is about human experiences,
not processes. Leadership is not a formula or a program;
it is a human activity that comes from the heart
and considers the hearts of others.

Lance Secretan

A leader cannot lead until he knows where he is going.

Anonymous

Good management is the art of making problems
so interesting and their solutions so constructive that
everyone wants to get to work and deal with them.

Paul Hawken

The final test of a leader is that he leaves behind him
in other men the conviction and the will to carry on.

Walter Lippmann

The greatness of a leader is measured by
the achievements of the led. This is the ultimate test
of his effectiveness.

Omar Bradley

The leadership instinct you are born with
is the backbone. You develop the funny bone
and the wishbone that go with it.

Elaine Agather

The best way to lead people into the future
is to connect with them deeply in the present.

James Kouzes and Barry Posner

Leadership is taking responsibility
while others are making excuses.

John C. Maxwell

To get others to come into our ways of thinking,
we must go over to theirs; and it is necessary to follow,
in order to lead.

William Hazlitt

How we think shows through in how we act.
Attitudes are mirrors of the mind. They reflect thinking.

David Joseph Schwartz

THE MEDIOCRE TEACHER TELLS.
THE GOOD TEACHER EXPLAINS.
THE SUPERIOR TEACHER
DEMONSTRATES. THE GREAT
TEACHER INSPIRES.

William Arthur Ward

Proper leadership empowers the workforce.
An empowered workforce means one that's committed,
that feels they're learning, that they're competent.
They have a sense of human bond, a sense of
community, a sense of meaning in their work.

Warren Bennis

Leaders must be close enough to relate to others,
but far enough ahead to motivate them.

John C. Maxwell

Leadership is a process whereby an individual influences
a group of individuals to achieve a common goal.

P.G. Northouse

The true teacher defends his pupils
against his own personal influence.

Amos Bronson Alcott

The mark of a great man is one who knows when to set aside the important things in order to accomplish the vital ones.

Brandon Sanderson

Successful leaders see the opportunities in every difficulty rather than the difficulty in every opportunity.

Reed Markham

Leadership is an ever-evolving position.

Mike Krzyzewski

True leadership lies in guiding others to success. In ensuring that everyone is performing at their best, doing the work they are pledged to do and doing it well.

Bill Owens

If we are to negotiate the coming years safely, we may need a new kind of leadership. To put it more precisely, we need the rediscovery of an ancient kind of leadership that has rarely been given the prominence it deserves. I mean the leader as teacher.

Jonathan Sacks

To know how to suggest is the great art of teaching.

Henri-Frédéric Amiel

Leadership is about being a servant first.

Allen West

Leadership has a harder job to do than just choosing sides. It must bring sides together.

Jesse Jackson

Nearly all men can stand adversity; but if you want
to test a man's character, give him power.

Abraham Lincoln

I believe we shall soon think of the leader as one
who organizes the experience of the group.

Mary Parker Follett

The role of leadership is to transform the complex
situation into small pieces and prioritize them.

Carlos Ghosn

For me, leadership is making a difference.
It's using your agency to bring about change.

Melanne Verveer

You have to recognize that every out-front maneuver
you make is going to be lonely, but if you feel entirely
comfortable, then you're not far enough ahead
to do any good. That warm sense of everything
going well is usually the body temperature
at the center of the herd.

John Masters

He who cannot be a good follower
cannot be a good leader.

Aristotle

Leadership is leaving something unsaid; the beholder is
given a chance to complete the idea and thus a great
masterpiece irresistibly rivets your attention
until you seem to become actually a part of it.

Okakura Kakuzō

It is hard to let old beliefs go. They are familiar. We are comfortable with them and have spent years building systems and developing habits that depend on them. Like a man who has worn eyeglasses so long that he forgets he has them on, we forget that the world looks to us the way it does because we have become used to seeing it that way through a particular set of lenses. Today, however, we need new lenses. And we need to throw the old ones away.

Kenichi Ohmae

That is what leadership is all about: staking your ground ahead of where opinion is and convincing people, not simply following the popular opinion of the moment.

Doris Kearns Goodwin

There is a great man who makes every man feel small. But the real great man is the man who makes every man feel great.

G.K. Chesterton

WHILE A GOOD LEADER
SUSTAINS MOMENTUM,
A GREAT LEADER INCREASES IT.

John C. Maxwell

One doesn't discover new lands without consenting
to lose sight of the shore for a very long time.

André Gide

Average leaders raise the bar on themselves;
good leaders raise the bar for others; great leaders
inspire others to raise their own bar.

Orrin Woodward

The most important thing about a commander
is his effect on morale.

Field Marshall Viscount Slim

To be trusted is a greater compliment than to be loved.

George MacDonald

To handle yourself, use your head.
To handle others, use your heart.

Donald Laird

If you wish your merit to be known,
acknowledge that of other people.

Oriental Proverb

There's no time to worry about keeping everybody
in line. Control is an illusion only achieved
when people are controlling themselves.

David Firth

Nothing is impossible for the man
who doesn't have to do it himself.

A.H. Weiler

Giving people self-confidence is by far the most important thing that I can do. Because then they will act.

Jack Welch

You don't lead by pointing and telling people some place to go. You lead by going to that place and making a case.

Ken Kesey

The true leader is always led.

Carl Jung

There is a moment just before success when, if we hesitate or try too hard, we will fail. Leadership is knowing the moments that will make you or break you.

Lolly Daskal

Being able to stay in a state of confusion until clarity
arrives is the height of intellectual ability.
It is what we call wisdom.

Trevor Bentley

Not the cry, but the flight of a wild duck,
leads the flock to fly and follow.

Chinese Proverb

A company is stronger if it is bound by love
rather than by fear.

Herb Kelleher

It's not a question of how much power you can hoard
for yourself, but how much you can give away.

Benjamin Zander

NEVER DOUBT THAT A SMALL
GROUP OF THOUGHTFUL,
CONCERNED CITIZENS
CAN CHANGE THE WORLD.
INDEED, IT IS THE ONLY THING
THAT EVER HAS.

Margaret Mead

Paradoxically, change seems to happen when you have
abandoned the chase after what you want to be
(or think you should be) and have accepted
— and fully experienced — what you are.

Janette Rainwater

To command is to serve, nothing more and nothing less.

André Malraux

You manage things; you lead people.

Rear Admiral Grace Murray Hopper

A great man shows his greatness
by the way he treats little men.

Thomas Carlyle

Wisdom equals knowledge plus courage. You have to not only know what to do and when to do it, but you have to also be brave enough to follow through.

Jarod Kintz

Before you are a leader, success is all about growing yourself. When you become a leader, success is all about growing others.

Jack Welch

There are two ways to get the tallest building in town. Tear everyone else's down or build your own up.

Anonymous

A wise leader remembers that people perceive service in their own terms and in their own expression.

Lolly Daskal

A skillful commander is not overbearing;
A skillful fighter does not become angry;
A skillful conqueror does not compete with people.
One who is skillful in using men
puts himself below them.
This is called the virtue of noncompeting.
This is called the strength to use men.
This is called matching Heaven.
The highest principle of old.

Lao Tzu

Leadership is relationships.

Benjamin Zander

The one important thing I have learned over the years
is the difference between taking one's work seriously
and taking one's self seriously. The first is imperative
and the second is disastrous.

Margot Fonteyn

The most successful leader of all is one
who sees another picture not yet actualized.

Mary Parker Follett

A person must learn to be adaptable and serve others
in order to rule. Willing followers are not acquired
by force or cunning but through consistency
in doing what is human and proper.

I Ching

A lot of people have great ideas, but a leader can take
a good idea and put it into successful action.

Lolly Daskal

A person can succeed at anything for which
there is enthusiasm.

Charles M. Schwab

Change is always a threat when done to people, but it's
embraced as an opportunity when done by people.

Rosabeth Moss Kanter

If you treat an individual as he is, he will remain
how he is. But if you treat him as if he were
what he ought to be and could be, he will become
what he ought to be and could be.

Goethe

All mankind is divided into three classes:
those that are immovable, those that are movable,
and those that move.

Benjamin Franklin

A good general not only sees the way to victory,
he also knows when victory is impossible.

Polybius

Outstanding leaders go out of their way to boost the self-esteem of their personnel. If people believe in themselves, it's amazing what they can accomplish.

Sam Walton

In this age, which believes there is a short cut to everything, the greatest lesson to be learned is that the most difficult way is, in the long run, the easiest.

Henry Miller

As a man thinketh in his heart, so is he.

King Solomon

Attitudes are more important than facts.

Karl Menninger

WE MUST ADJUST TO CHANGING
TIMES AND STILL HOLD TO
UNCHANGING PRINCIPLES.

Jimmy Carter

A true leader has the confidence to stand alone,
the courage to make tough decisions,
and the compassion to listen to the needs of others.
He does not set out to be a leader, but becomes one by
the equality of his actions and the integrity of his intent.

Douglas MacArthur

The leader has to be practical and a realist, yet must
talk the language of the visionary and the idealist.

Eric Hoffer

A man who wants to lead the orchestra
must turn his back on the crowd.

Max Lucado

As we look ahead into the next century,
leaders will be those who empower others.

Bill Gates

Deal with the faults of others as gently as with your own.

Chinese Proverb

Don't necessarily avoid sharp edges.
Occasionally they are necessary to leadership.

Donald Rumsfeld

Don't find fault, find a remedy.

Henry Ford

Don't be afraid to give up the good to go for the great.

John D. Rockefeller

The difference between great and average
or lousy in any job is, mostly, having the imagination
and zeal to re-create yourself daily.

Tom Peters

A genuine leader is not a searcher for consensus
but a molder of consensus.

Martin Luther King Jr.

Great leaders are not defined by the absence of
weakness, but rather by the presence of clear strengths.

John Zenger

You must be the change that you wish to see
in the world.

Mahatma Gandhi

Great leaders are almost always great simplifiers,
who can cut through argument, debate, and doubt
to offer a solution everybody can understand.

Colin Powell

Make yourself indispensable, and you will move up.
Act as though you are indispensable,
and you will move out.

Jules Ormont

He who has great power should use it lightly.

Seneca

I cannot give you the formula for success,
but I can give you the formula for failure, which is:
Try to please everybody.

Herbert Swope

A man who works with his hands is a laborer.
A man who works with his hands and his brains
is a craftsman. But a man who works with his hands
and his brain and his heart is an artist.

Louis Nizer

LEADERSHIP: CONVERTING DREAMS INTO GOALS AND GOALS INTO SUCCESS.

Lolly Daskal

If you don't think of yourself as a leader, then you're limited in your thinking. Leading is the way we help move people into action, including ourselves. The question is not whether you are a leader, but how well you lead.

Bruce D. Schneider

If one is lucky, a solitary fantasy can totally transform one million realities.

Maya Angelou

An individual without information can't take responsibility. An individual with information can't help but take responsibility.

Jan Carlzon

Never give an order that can't be obeyed.

Douglas MacArthur

Effort and courage are not enough
without purpose and direction.

John F. Kennedy

Energy and perseverance can fit a man
for almost any kind of position.

Theodore F. Merseles

In matters of style, swim with the current;
in matters of principle, stand like a rock.

Thomas Jefferson

When the wind blows, some people build walls,
others build windmills.

Peter Hawkins

Lead and inspire people. Don't try to manage
and manipulate people. Inventories can be managed
but people must be led.

Ross Perot

Leadership does not always wear
the harness of compromise.

Woodrow Wilson

Great leadership is about lifting people up
when they don't know they have wings.

Lolly Daskal

No man is good enough to govern another man
without that other's consent.

Abraham Lincoln

There is timing in the whole life of the warrior, in his thriving and declining, in his harmony and discord. Similarly, there is timing in the Way of the merchant, in the rise and fall of capital. All things entail rising and falling timing. You must be able to discern this.

Miyamoto Musashi

Four steps to achievement: Plan purposefully. Prepare prayerfully. Proceed positively. Pursue persistently

William A. Ward

It takes twenty years to make an overnight success.

Eddie Cantor

We've got to learn to live with chaos and uncertainty, to try to be comfortable with it and not to look for certainty where we won't get it.

Charles Handy

What you do has far greater impact than what you say.

Stephen Covey

It is the greatest mistake to think that man is always one
and the same. A man is never the same for long.
He is continually changing. He seldom remains
the same even for half an hour.

George Gurdjieff

Though I might travel afar, I will meet only what I carry
with me, for every man is a mirror. We see only
ourselves reflected in those around us. Their attitudes
and actions are only a reflection of our own.
The whole world and its condition has its counterparts
within us all. Turn the gaze inward. Correct yourself
and the world will change.

Kirsten Zambucka

The great accomplishments of man have resulted from
the transmission of ideas and enthusiasm.

Thomas Watson Jr.

Great minds must be ready not only to
take opportunities, but to make them.

C.C. Colton

Great works are performed not by strength
but by perseverance.

Samuel Johnson

Give every man thy ear, but few thy voice.

William Shakespeare

HARD WORK WITHOUT TALENT
IS A SHAME,

BUT TALENT WITHOUT
HARD WORK IS A TRAGEDY.

Robert Half

I've got to follow them; I am their leader.

Alexandre Ledru-Rollin

I always prefer to believe the best of everybody;
it saves so much trouble.

Rudyard Kipling

Leadership is seeing people not as they are,
but as who they can become.

Lolly Daskal

There are two ways of being creative. One can sing
and dance. Or one can create an environment
in which singers and dancers flourish.

Warren Bennis

Whatever you are, be a good one.

Abraham Lincoln

I am a great believer in luck, and I find the harder
I work, the more I have of it.

Stephen Leacock

I can give you a six-word formula for success:
Think things through, then follow through.

Edward Rickenbacker

I can live for two months on a good compliment.

Mark Twain

I cannot teach anybody anything;
I can only make them think.

Socrates

To have long-term success as a coach or in any position
of leadership, you have to be obsessed in some way.

Pat Riley

We live in a society obsessed with public opinion.
But leadership has never been about popularity.

Marco Rubio

As a leader, the greatest good we can do for others
is not to share our riches, but to reveal theirs.

Lolly Daskal

You gain strength, courage and confidence by every experience in which you really stop to look fear in the face.... You must do the thing you think you cannot do.

Eleanor Roosevelt

A competent leader can get efficient service from poor troops, while on the contrary an incapable leader can demoralize the best of troops.

John J. Pershing

Getting good players is easy.
Getting them to play together is the hard part.

Casey Stengel

We will either find a way or make one.

Hannibal

MAN DOESN'T KNOW
WHAT HE IS CAPABLE OF
UNTIL HE IS ASKED.

Kofi Annan

I am a leader by default only because nature
does not allow a vacuum.

Bishop Desmond Tutu

Take a chance! All life is a chance. The man who goes
furthest is generally the one who is willing to do and
dare. The sure-thing boat never gets far from shore.

Dale Carnegie

Example is not the main thing in influencing others.
It is the only thing.

Albert Schweitzer

Every new adjustment is a crisis in self-esteem.

Eric Hoffer

It is always the simple that produces the marvelous.

Amelia Barr

No man will make a great leader who wants to do it all himself or get all the credit for doing it.

Andrew Carnegie

Tell everyone what you want to do
and someone will want to help you do it.

W. Clement Stone

More will be accomplished, and better,
and with more ease, if every man does what he
is best fitted to do, and nothing else.

Plato

Character may almost be called the most effective means of persuasion.

Aristotle

Know or listen to those who know.

Balthazar Gracián

To become truly great, one has to stand with people, not above them.

Montesquieu

He who is to be a good ruler must have first been ruled.

Aristotle

If you would persuade, you must appeal
to interest rather than intellect.

Benjamin Franklin

No one can whistle a symphony.
It takes an orchestra to play it.

Halford E. Luccock

We are not put on this earth for ourselves,
but are placed here for each other.
If you are there always for others, then in time of need,
someone will be there for you.

Jeff Warner

If there be any truer measure of a man than
by what he does, it must be by what he gives.

Bishop Robert South

I believe much trouble and blood would be saved
if we opened our hearts more.

Chief Joseph

Done is better than perfect.

Sheryl Sandberg

There are two ways of spreading light:
to be the candle or the mirror that reflects it.

Edith Wharton

One of the best ways to persuade others is with your ears
— by listening to them.

Dean Rusk

Never leave that till tomorrow which you can do today.

Benjamin Franklin

We don't want people who are satisfied with the way
things are. We want people who are curious,
impatient, and who are constantly trying to buck
the trend of received wisdom.

C.K. Prahalad

The greatest compliment that was ever paid me
was when one asked me what I thought,
and attended to my answer.

Henry David Thoreau

Everyone is needed but no one is necessary.

Bruce Coslet

HIRE THE BEST. PAY THEM FAIRLY.
COMMUNICATE FREQUENTLY.
PROVIDE CHALLENGES AND
REWARDS. BELIEVE IN THEM.
GET OUT OF THEIR WAY AND
THEY'LL KNOCK YOUR SOCKS OFF.

Mary Ann Allison

My main job was developing talent. I was a gardener
providing water and other nourishment to our top
750 people. Of course, I had to pull out some weeds, too.

Jack Welch

Governing a large organization requires timely activity
and discreet inactivity on the part of the leader.
One must be particularly sensitive to promising
circumstances, talented men and the right objectives.

I Ching

Surround yourself with the best people you can find,
delegate authority, and don't interfere as long as
the policy you've decided upon is being carried out.

Ronald Reagan

One of the best ways to lead people is to lead with heart.

Lolly Daskal

Everything in the world we want to do or get done,
we must do with and through people.

Earl Nightingale

The chief lesson I have learned in a long life is that the
only way you can make a man trustworthy is to trust
him; and the surest way to make him untrustworthy
is to distrust him and show your distrust.

Henry Stimson

You don't lead by hitting people over the head —
that's assault, not leadership.

Dwight Eisenhower

You cannot mandate productivity; you must
provide the tools to let people become their best.

Steve Jobs

Trust each other again and again. When the trust level
gets high enough, people transcend apparent limits,
discovering new and awesome abilities
of which they were previously unaware.

David Armistead

Motivation is everything. You can do the work
of two people, but you can't be two people.
Instead, you have to inspire the next guy down the line
and get him to inspire his people.

Lee Iacocca

Leaders in the new organization do not lack
motivational tools, but the tools are different from those
of traditional corporate bureaucrats. The new rewards
are based not on status but on contribution, and they
consist not of regular promotion and automatic
pay rises, but of excitement about the mission
and a share of the glory of success.

Rosabeth Moss Kanter

Never confuse motion with action.

Benjamin Franklin

In order that people are happy in their work,
these three things are needed: they must be fit for it;
they must not do too much of it; and they must have a
sense of success in it — not a doubtful success,
such as needs some testimony of others for its
confirmation, but a sure sense, or rather, knowledge,
that so much work has been done well and fruitfully
done, whatever the world may say or think about it.

W.H. Auden

Of course, we all have our limits, but how can you
possibly find your boundaries unless you explore as far
and as wide as you possibly can? I would rather fail
in an attempt at something new and uncharted than
safely succeed in a repeat of something I have done.

A.E. Hotchner

THOSE THAT KNOW, DO.
THOSE THAT UNDERSTAND,
TEACH.

Aristotle

Just because we are all equal doesn't mean
we're all the same.

Anonymous

Some people change their ways when they see the light,
others when they feel the heat.

Caroline Schroeder

The best kind of leadership comes from the heart.

Lolly Daskal

The only person I control in the entire world is me.
People work in their own best interests, not mine.
It used to be that my people were responsible to me.
Now I am responsible to them.

Ralph Stayer

When people lead, they shouldn't have to leave their hearts at home.

Lolly Daskal

Making people do what you think they ought to do does not lead to clarity and consciousness. While they may do what you tell them to at any time, they will inwardly cringe, grow confused and plot revenge.

Erving and Miriam Polster

The secret of education lies in respecting the pupil.

Ralph Waldo Emerson

Set your expectations high; find men and women whose integrity and values you respect; get their agreement on a course of action; and give them your ultimate trust.

John Akers

You can buy a person's hand, but you can't buy his heart. His heart is where his enthusiasm, his loyalty is. You can buy his back, but you can't buy his brain. That's where his creativity is, his ingenuity, his resourcefulness.

Stephen Covey

You can buy someone's time, you can buy someone's physical presence at a given place, you can even buy a measured number of skilled muscular motions per hour or day. But you cannot buy enthusiasm, you cannot buy initiative, you cannot buy loyalty, you cannot buy devotion of hearts, minds, and souls. You have to earn these things.

Clarence Francis

We must not, in trying to think about how we can make a big difference, ignore the small daily differences we can make which, over time, add up to big differences that we often cannot foresee.

Marian Wright Edelman

I don't like work — no man does — but I like what is in work — the chance to find yourself. Your own reality — for yourself, not others — what no other man can ever know.

Joseph Conrad

Understanding and accepting diversity enables us to see that each of us is needed. It also enables us to begin to think about being abandoned to the strengths of others, and admitting that we cannot know or do everything.

Max De Pree

My grandfather once told me that there were two kinds
of people; those who do the work and those who take
the credit. He told me to try to be in the first group;
there was much less competition.

Indira Gandhi

Be daring, be different, be impractical, be anything that
will assert integrity of purpose and imaginative vision
against the play-it-safers, the creatures of the
commonplace, the slaves of the ordinary.

Cecil Beaton

Life can either be accepted or changed. If it is not
accepted, it must be changed. If it cannot be changed,
then it must be accepted.

Winston Churchill

The most important choice you make is
what you choose to make important.

Michael Neill

Every man who rises above the common level has
received two educations: the first from his teachers;
the second, more personal and important, from himself.

Edward Gibbon

The greatest gift you can give another
is the purity of your attention.

Richard Moss

Allow regular time for silent reflection.
Turn inward and digest what has happened.
Let the senses rest and grow still.

John Heider

WE ARE ALL VALUABLE,
WE JUST HAVE TO DECIDE
HOW WE WILL ADD VALUE.

Lolly Daskal

Three of the key elements in the art of working together are how to deal with change, how to deal with conflict, and how to reach our potential....the needs of the team are best met when we meet the needs of individual persons.

Max De Pree

Saying smart things and giving smart answers are important. Learning to listen to others and to ask smart questions is more important.

Bob Sutton

Champions aren't made in gyms, champions are made from something they have deep inside them — a desire, a dream, a vision. They have to have last-minute stamina, they have to be a little faster, they have to have the skill and the will. But the will must be stronger than the skill.

Muhammad Ali

Confusion is a word we have invented for an order
which is not understood.

Henry Miller

The true test of character is not how much
we know how to do, but how we behave
when we don't know what to do.

John Holt

Leadership is giving out far more
than one expects in direct return.

Lolly Daskal

The wise facilitator's ability does not rest on techniques
or gimmicks or set exercises. Become aware of process
— and when you see this clearly, you can shed light
on the process for others.

The Tao Te Ching

One looks back with appreciation to the brilliant teachers, but with gratitude to those who touched our human feeling.

Carl Jung

A good listener tries to understand what the other person is saying. In the end he may disagree sharply, but because he disagrees, he wants to know exactly what it is he is disagreeing with.

Kenneth A. Wells

The leader judges no one and is attentive to both 'good' and 'bad' people.

John Heider

It is wrong to coerce people into opinions, but it is our duty to impel them into experiences.

Kurt Hahn

The biggest obstacle to learning something new
is the belief that you already know it.

Zen Philosophy

A man of character finds a special attractiveness in
difficulty, since it is only by coming to grips with
difficulty that he can realize his own potentialities.

Charles de Gaulle

We never get to the bottom of ourselves on our own.
We discover who we are face to face and side by side
with others in work, love, and learning.

Robert Bellah

The task of leadership is to create an alignment of strengths
so strong that it makes the system's weaknesses irrelevant.

Peter Drucker

THE BEST TEST OF A PERSON'S
CHARACTER IS HOW
HE OR SHE TREATS THOSE
WITH LESS POWER.

Bob Sutton

What we call leadership consists mainly of knowing
how to follow. The wise leader stays in the background
and facilitates other people's process.

John Heider

My father used to say to me, "Whenever you get into
a jam, whenever you get into a crisis or an emergency...
become the calmest person in the room
and you'll be able to figure your way out of it."

Rudolph Giuliani

No man is wise enough by himself.

Plautus

A wise leader allows people to be who they are and
bring their strength and talents to everything they do.

Lolly Daskal

The great leaders are like the best conductors — they
reach beyond the notes to reach the magic in the players.

Blaine Lee

Like people without worrying
if they are going to like you in return.

Burt Reynolds

All growth is a leap in the dark, a spontaneous,
unpremeditated act without benefit of experience.

Henry Miller

Through others we become ourselves.

Lev Vygotsky

Work and self-worth are the two factors in pride
that interact with each other and that tend to increase
the strong sense of pride found in superior work teams.
When people do something of obvious worth,
they feel a strong sense of personal worth.

Dennis Kinlaw

Taking action on a good leadership idea is better than
just speaking about having a good leadership idea.

Lolly Daskal

Your behavior influences others through a ripple effect.
A ripple effect works because everyone influences
everyone else. Powerful people are powerful influences.

John Heider

People will always want a leader that can show them the way, not a leader that commands the way.

Lolly Daskal

The more I am open to the realities in me
and in the other person, the less do I find myself
wishing to rush in to "fix things."

Carl Rogers

A green light means, "Yes, we want you to feel free to
open up, ask questions, take charge, find new ways."
A red light means, "No, we don't want that."
High productivity comes when people are allowed
to be productive, take initiative, develop creative
solutions and produce results.

Bob Basso

When I give up trying to impress the group, I become very impressive. But when I am just trying to make myself look good, the group knows that and does not like it.

The Tao Te Ching

Tolerance is the positive and cordial effort to understand another's beliefs, practices, and habits without necessarily sharing or accepting them.

Joshua Liebman

When spiders unite, they can tie down a lion.

African Proverb

Creativity can be described as letting go of certainties.

Gail Sheehy

Life's fulfillment finds constant obstacles in its path;
but those are necessary for the sake of its advance.
The stream is saved from the sluggishness of its
current by the perpetual opposition of the soil through
which it must cut its way. The spirit of fight
belongs to the genius of life.

Rabindranath Tagore

I think the leader on the dogsled is the lead dog,
not the guy on the back with the whip.

John Chambers

The great rivers and seas are kings of all mountain
streams because they skillfully stay below them.
That is why they can be their kings. Therefore,
in order to be the superior of the people, one must,
in the use of words, place himself below them,
and in order to be ahead of the people, one must,
in one's own person, follow them.

Lao Tzu

ALL THE ART OF LIVING
LIES IN A FINE MINGLING OF
LETTING GO AND HOLDING ON.

Havelock Ellis

If you want to build a ship, don't drum up people together to collect wood and don't assign them tasks and work, but rather teach them to long for the endless immensity of the sea.

Antoine de Saint-Exupéry

The way to make people shine is to let them be the gems that they are, and just provide a good setting and a little polish.

Anonymous

Leadership is more about purpose than it's about position.

Lolly Daskal

There is great force hidden in a gentle command.

George Herbert

The leaders who work most effectively, it seems to me,
never say "I." And that's not because they have trained
themselves not to say "I." They don't think "I."
They think "we"; they think "team." They understand
their job to be to make the team function.
They accept responsibility and don't sidestep it,
but "we" gets the credit....This is what creates trust,
what enables you to get the task done.

Peter Drucker

The new model of leadership is partially a result of the
decline of the command-and-control style organization.
It is a learn-and-lead model, in which leaders are
continuous learners. They are open and always listening
as they develop a vision and then motivate their staff
to turn that vision into business reality.
Companies that develop leaders at all levels
are going to reap the benefits while those
that lag behind will be forced to play catch-up.

Edward Wakin

The mediocre leader tells. The good leader explains. The superior leader demonstrates. The great leader inspires.

Steve Buchholz and Thomas Roth

Great discoveries and improvements invariably involve the cooperation of many minds.

Alexander Graham Bell

There are two primary ways in which man relates himself to the world that surrounds him: manipulation and appreciation. In the first way he sees in what surrounds him things to be handled, forces to be managed, objects to be put to use. In the second way he sees in what surrounds him things to be acknowledged, understood, valued or admired.

Abraham Joshua Heschel

The essence of leadership is the capacity to build
and develop the self-esteem of the workers.

Irwin Federman

In the long history of humankind (and animal kind, too)
those who learned to collaborate and improvise
most effectively have prevailed.

Charles Darwin

Leadership is not the private reserve of a few charismatic
men and women. It is a process ordinary managers
use when they are bringing forth the best
from themselves and others.

James Kouzes and Barry Posner

IF YOU'RE RIDIN' AHEAD OF
THE HERD, TAKE A LOOK BACK
EVERY NOW AND THEN TO
MAKE SURE IT'S STILL THERE.

The Cowboy's Guide to Life

Truly great leaders spend as much time collecting
and acting upon feedback as they do providing it.

Alexander Lucia

Coaching isn't an addition to a leader's job.
It's an integral part of it.

George S. Odiorne

In a period of rapid change, something stable is needed
in organizations. That's what culture is for. It's the
stick-gum that holds the group together because it tells
everybody involved, this is how we like to operate.

Tom McDonald

When I let go of what I am, I become what I might be.

Lolly Daskal

We herd sheep, we drive cattle, we lead people.
Lead me, follow me, or get out of my way.

George S. Patton

Leaders aren't born, they are made. And they are made
just like anything else, through hard work.
And that's the price we'll have to pay
to achieve that goal, or any goal.

Vince Lombardi

Bosses create fear, leaders exude confidence.
Bosses fix blame, leaders correct mistakes.
Bosses know all, leaders ask questions.
Bosses make work menial,
leaders make work interesting.
Bosses are interested in themselves,
leaders are interested in others.

Lolly Daskal

No institution can possibly survive if it needs geniuses
or supermen to manage it. It must be organized
in such a way as to be able to get along under
a leadership composed of average human beings.

Peter Drucker

If you're in charge and you stop rowing,
don't be surprised if the rest of your crew stops too.

Anonymous

To be a catalyst is the ambition most appropriate
for those who see the world as being in constant change,
and who, without thinking that they can control it,
wish to influence its direction.

Theodore Zeldin

Run an honest, open group. The fewer rules the better. Every law creates an outlaw. Good leadership means doing less and being more.

The Tao Te Ching

Do you want to be a positive influence in the world? First, get your own life in order. Ground yourself in the single principle so that your behavior is wholesome and effective. If you do that, you will earn respect and be a powerful influence.

John Heider

He that would govern others, first should be the master of himself, richly endowed with depth of understanding, height of courage and those remarkable graces which I dare not ascribe unto myself.

Philip Massinger

The kind of conversation I like is one in which you are
prepared to emerge a slightly different person.

Theodore Zeldin

The leader is always learning new things
and gaining new insights.

Lolly Daskal

In really good companies, you have to lead. You have to
come up with big ideas and express them forcefully.
I have always been encouraged, or sometimes forced,
to confront the very natural fear of being wrong.
I was constantly pushed to find out what I really
thought and then to speak up. Over time, I came to see
that waiting to discover which way the wind was
blowing is an excellent way to learn how to be a follower.

Roger Enrico

Leadership is about taking an organization to a place
it would not otherwise have gone without you,
in a value-adding, measurable way.

George M.C. Fisher

A true leader always keeps an element of surprise
up his sleeve, which others cannot grasp but which
keeps his public excited and breathless.

Charles de Gaulle

I have three precious things which I hold fast and prize.
The first is gentleness; the second is frugality; the third is
humility, which keeps me from putting myself before
others. Be gentle and you can be bold; be frugal and you
can be liberal; avoid putting yourself before others,
and you can become a leader among men.

Lao Tzu

TO BE HUMBLE TO SUPERIORS
IS DUTY; TO EQUALS, COURTESY;
TO INFERIORS, NOBLENESS.

Benjamin Franklin

Courage is the main quality of leadership, in my opinion,
no matter where it is exercised. Usually it implies
some risk — especially in new undertakings.
Courage to initiate something and to keep it going —
pioneering and adventurous spirit to blaze new ways.

Walt Disney

The vision must be followed by the venture. It is not
enough to stare up the steps. We must step up the stairs.

Vance Havner

Leadership is not just a privilege, but a responsibility.

Lolly Daskal

I will not follow where the path may lead, but I will go
where there is no path, and I will leave a trail.

Muriel Strode

Union does everything when it is perfect. It satisfies
desires, it simplifies needs, it foresees the wishes
of the imagination; it is an aisle always open,
and becomes a constant fortune.

Étienne Pivert de Senancour

It is amazing what you can accomplish
if you do not care who gets the credit.

Harry Truman

One analogy [for the manager] is the conductor
of a symphony orchestra, through whose effort,
vision and leadership, individual instrumental parts
that are so much noise by themselves, become
the living whole of music. But the conductor
has the composer's score: he is only interpreter.
The manager is both composer and conductor.

Peter Drucker

Coming together is a beginning. Keeping together is progress. Working together is success.

Henry Ford

Leadership is working with goals and vision; management is working with objectives.

Russel Honoré

Never criticize a man until you've walked a mile in his moccasins.

Native American Proverb

Never believe anything bad about anybody unless you positively know it to be true; never tell even that unless you feel that it is absolutely necessary — and remember that God is listening while you tell it.

Henry Van Dyke

If I could solve all the problems myself, I would.

Thomas Edison

You've got to enthuse the people who do the work.
You can't light a bonfire at the top. It only happens
when you light the fire at the bottom.

Alistair Cummings

Be willing to take a stand for things you believe in,
because no one else will stand there for you.

Lolly Daskal

We judge ourselves by what we feel capable of doing,
while others judge us by what we have already done.

Henry Wadsworth Longfellow

IT'S NOT WHAT YOU ARE THAT
HOLDS YOU BACK, IT'S WHAT
YOU THINK YOU ARE NOT.

Denis Waitley

I am personally convinced that one person can be
a change catalyst, a "transformer," in any situation,
any organization. Such an individual is yeast that can
leaven an entire loaf. It requires vision, initiative,
patience, respect, persistence, courage,
and faith to be a transforming leader.

Stephen Covey

Leaders are essentially visualizers and actualizers. They
can visualize something and actually make it happen.

Lolly Daskal

It is the capacity to link the values and beliefs
of the leader with the needs, goals, values and beliefs
of the followers that is the magic of leadership.

John Hunt

What I've really learned over time is that optimism
is a very, very important part of leadership.

Bob Iger

The business of the samurai consists in reflecting
on his own station in life, in discharging loyal service
to his master if he has one, in deepening his fidelity
in association with his friends and,
with due consideration of his own position,
in devoting himself to duty above all.

Yamaga Sokō

We're like blind men on a corner. We have to learn to
trust people or we'll never cross the street.

George Foreman

When something bad happens to you,
you have three choices. You can let it:
Destroy you
Define you
Develop you.

Lolly Daskal

No leader sets out to be a leader. People set out to
live their lives, expressing themselves fully.
When their expression is of value, they become leaders.

Warren Bennis

Motivation is like food for the brain. You cannot
get enough in one sitting. It needs continual
and regular top-ups.

Peter Davies

A leader has a vision and conviction that a dream
can be achieved. He inspires the power
and energy to get it done.

Ralph Lauren

The bravest are surely those who have the clearest vision
of what is before them, glory and danger alike,
and yet notwithstanding, go out to meet it.

Thucydides

People ask the difference between a leader and a boss.
The leader works in the open, and the boss in covert.
The leader leads, and the boss drives.

Theodore Roosevelt

What makes a multitude of individuals a society
rather than a crowd is a commonly held ideal.

Melvin Lyon

When written in Chinese, the word "crisis" is composed
of two characters. One represents danger
and the other represents opportunity.

John F. Kennedy

We must, indeed, all hang together, or most assuredly,
we shall hang separately.

Benjamin Franklin

You cannot live a positive life with a negative attitude.

Lolly Daskal

Make a careful list of all the things done to you that
you abhorred. Don't do them to others, ever.
Make another list of things done for you that you loved.
Do them for others always.

Dee Hock

Character is doing what's right when nobody's looking.

J.C. Watts

The real leader has no need to lead —
he is content to point the way.

Henry Miller

The biggest step in changing the world around you
is to change the world within you.

Lolly Daskal

Leadership consists not in degrees of technique but in
traits of character; it requires moral rather than athletic
or intellectual effort, and it imposes on both leader and
follower alike the burdens of self-restraint.

Lewis H. Lapham

LEADERSHIP OFFERS AN
OPPORTUNITY TO MAKE
A DIFFERENCE IN SOMEONE'S
LIFE, NO MATTER WHAT
THE PROJECT.

Bill Owens

Where there is unity, there is always victory.

Publilius Syrus

Leadership is bringing people into
new realms of excellence and challenging them
to become distinguished.

Lolly Daskal

Leadership is about doing what you know is right —
even when a growing din of voices around you is trying
to convince you to accept what you know to be wrong.

Robert. L. Ehrlich

I think the greater responsibility, in terms of morality,
is where leadership begins.

Norman Lear

Actions, not words, are the ultimate results
of leadership.... Leadership is an active role;
"lead" is a verb. But the leader who tries to do it all
is headed for burnout, and in a powerful hurry.

Bill Owens

You can't get ahead while you are getting even.

Dick Armey

Now there are five matters to which a general must pay
strict heed. The first of these is administration;
the second, preparedness; the third, determination;
the fourth, prudence; and the fifth, economy.

Wu Ch'i

Love does not consist in gazing at each other but in
looking outward together in the same direction.

Antoine de Saint-Exupéry

Unity requires a collective moral force,
together with a great leader.

I Ching

We cannot be a source of strength
unless we nurture our own strength.

Lolly Daskal

Leadership means forming a team and working
toward common objectives that are tied to time,
metrics, and resources.

Russel Honoré

What it lies in our power to do,
it lies in our power not to do.

Aristotle

Make it a point to do something every day that you don't want to do. This is the golden rule for acquiring the habit of doing your duty without pain.

Mark Twain

The common denominator of success —
the secret of every man who has ever been successful —
lies in the fact that he formed the habit of doing things
that failures don't like to do.

Albert Gray

When he took the time to help the man
up the mountain, lo, he scaled it himself.

Anonymous

People look for their leadership to lead.

Mick Cornett

THE MIRACLE IS THIS:
THE MORE WE SHARE,
THE MORE WE HAVE.

Leonard Nimoy

I believe that the will of the people is resolved by
a strong leadership. Even in a democratic society, events
depend on a strong leadership with a strong power of
persuasion, and not on the opinion of the masses.

Yitzhak Shamir

The world is starving for original
and decisive leadership.

Bryant McGill

Men acquire a particular quality by constantly acting
a particular way.... You become just by performing
just actions, temperate by performing temperate actions,
brave by performing brave actions.

Aristotle

The one thing I have learned as a CEO is that
leadership at various levels is vastly different.
When I was leading a function or a business, there were
certain demands and requirements to be a leader.
As you move up the organization, the requirements
for leading that organization don't grow vertically;
they grow exponentially.

Indra Nooyi

The self is not something ready-made, but something
in continuous formation through choice of action.

John Dewey

Many individuals have, like uncut diamonds,
shining qualities beneath a rough exterior.

Juvenal

It is in men as in soils where sometimes there
is a vein of gold which the owner knows not of.

Jonathan Swift

The true portrait of a man is a fusion of what
he thinks he is, what others think he is,
what he really is and what he tries to be.

Dore Schary

He who knows much about others may be learned,
but he who understands himself is more intelligent.
He who controls others may be powerful,
but he who has mastered himself is mightier still.

Lao Tzu

The speed of the boss is the speed of the team.

Lee Iacocca

In the military, I learned that "leadership" means raising your hand and volunteering for the tough, important assignments.

Tulsi Gabbard

Let there be spaces in your togetherness.

Kahlil Gibran

None of us is as smart as all of us.

Anonymous

Rather than focusing on things you cannot change, focus on the things you can.

Lolly Daskal

Upon the conduct of each depends the fate of all.

Alexander the Great

One person with a belief is equal to
a force of 99 who have only interests.

John Stuart Mill

A leader must not only be willing to give opportunity
to others, but must be in the business of creating
opportunity for others.

William Hodges

Many ideas grow better when transplanted into another
mind than in the one where they sprang up.

Oliver Wendell Holmes

It is not so much our friends' help that helps us,
as the confidence of their help.

Epicurus

A key characteristic of transformational leaders
is that they motivate people to do more
than they originally expected to.

Elizabeth Chell

I not only use all the brains I have, but all I can borrow.

Woodrow Wilson

Always try to do something for the other fellow and you
will be agreeably surprised how things come your way
— how many pleasing things are done for you.

Claude M. Bristol

THE NEXT TIME YOU'RE IN A
MEETING, LOOK AROUND AND
IDENTIFY THE YES-BUTTERS,
THE NOT-KNOWERS AND THE
WHY-NOTTERS. WHY-NOTTERS
MOVE THE WORLD.

Louise Pierson

The ultimate leader is one who is willing to develop
people to the point that they eventually surpass
him or her in knowledge and ability.

Fred A. Manske, Jr.

Love all. Serve all. Help all.

Lolly Daskal

There can only be one state of mind as you approach
any profound test: total concentration,
a spirit of togetherness, and strength.

Pat Riley

When your work speaks for itself, don't interrupt.

Henry Kaiser

Men are not to be judged by their looks, habits and appearances; but by the character of their lives and conversations, and by their works.

Sir Roger L'Estrange

Don't mind criticism. If it is untrue, disregard it; if unfair, keep from irritation; if it is ignorant, smile; if it is justified, it is not criticism — learn from it.

Anonymous

Call it a clan,
call it a network,
call it a tribe,
call it a family.
Whatever you call it,
whoever you are,
you need one.

Jane Howard

There is no such thing as a self-made man. You will reach your goals only with the help of others.

George Shinn

No one lives long enough to learn everything they need to learn starting from scratch. To be successful, we absolutely, positively have to find people who have already paid the price to learn the things that we need to learn to achieve our goals.

Brian Tracy

Be the kind of person that you want to meet.

Lolly Daskal

To belittle is to be little.

Anonymous

You were born to win, but to be a winner, you must plan to win, prepare to win, and expect to win.

Zig Ziglar

You'll do more good if you aim to serve more than you aim to please.

Chris Edmonds

Leadership is a journey. Each one of us has to take our own path, and get there our own way.

David Gergen

How you come across to others is too important to be left to chance.

Phil Geldart

I ASKED, "WHY DOESN'T
SOMEBODY DO SOMETHING?"
THEN I REALIZED
I WAS SOMEBODY.

Anonymous

Never wonder why you are not like others.
Live in such a way that you make others wonder
why they are not like you.

Lolly Daskal

Tell me and I'll forget; show me and I may remember;
involve me and I'll understand.

Chinese Proverb

I know the price of success: dedication, hard work,
and an unremitting devotion to the things
you want to see happen.

Frank Lloyd Wright

Only the man who can impose discipline on himself is fit
to discipline others or can impose discipline on others.

William Feather

I praise loudly; I blame softly.

Catherine the Great

Your most valuable asset in learning
is a positive attitude.

Bobbi DePorter

Leadership is an acquired taste —
not for the faint of heart.

Lolly Daskal

You cannot teach a man anything.
You can only help him to find it within himself.

Galileo Galilei

It does not take much strength to do things, but it requires a great deal of strength to decide what to do.

Elbert Hubbard

The one thing we can never get enough of is love; and the one thing we never give enough of is love.

Henry Miller

Be patient with everyone, but above all with yourself. I mean do not be disheartened by your imperfections, but always rise up with fresh courage. How are we to be patient in dealing with our neighbor's faults if we are impatient in dealing with our own?

Francis de Sales

He who stops being better stops being good.

Oliver Cromwell

Never cease to be convinced that life might be better — your own and others'.

André Gide

One may be better than his reputation or his conduct but never better than his principles.

Nicolas V. De Latena

The pleasure of love is in loving. We are happier in the passion we feel than in that which we excite.

La Rochefoucauld

Strong lives are motivated by dynamic purposes.

Kenneth Hildebrand

Thinking is easy, acting is difficult,
and to put one's thoughts into action
is the most difficult thing in the world.

Goethe

To give yourself the best possible chance of playing
to your potential, you must prepare for
every eventuality. That means practice.

Steve Ballesteros

If each of us hires people who are smaller than we are,
we shall become a company of dwarfs.
But if each of us hires people who are bigger than we are,
we shall become a company of giants.

David Ogilvy

We are what we repeatedly do.
Excellence, then, is not, an act, but a habit.

Will Durant

Get the best people and train them well.

Scott McNealy

Our business in life is not to get ahead of others,
but to get ahead of ourselves.

E. Joseph Cossman

The practice of patience toward one another,
the overlooking of one another's defects, and the bearing
of one another's burdens is the most elementary
condition of all human and social activity in the family,
in the professions, and in society.

Lawrence G. Lovasik

LEADERSHIP IS
MAKING THE WISE DECISION
EVEN WHEN IT'S HARD.

Lolly Daskal

Good enough never is.

Debbi Fields

Great companies, in the way they work,
start with great leaders.

Steve Ballmer

Leadership is serving people with your whole heart
with everyone you meet and with everything that you do.

Lolly Daskal

To look is one thing. To see what you look at is another.
To understand what you see is a third. To learn from
what you understand is still something else.
But to act on what you learn is all that really matters.

Anonymous

A leader isn't someone who forces others
to make him stronger; a leader is someone willing
to give his strength to others so that they may have
the strength to stand on their own.

Beth Revis

Life isn't easy, and leadership is harder still.

Walter Russell Mead

I don't see myself being special; I just see myself
having more responsibilities than the next man.
People look to me to do things for them, to have answers.

Tupac Shakur

Strong convictions precede great actions.

James Freeman Clarke

Leadership appears to be the art of getting others to
want to do something you are convinced should be done.

Vance Packard

If you would convince a man that he does wrong,
do right. But do not care to convince him.
Men will believe what they see. Let them see.

Henry David Thoreau

I cannot trust a man to control others
who cannot control himself.

Robert E. Lee

What government is best? That which teaches us
to govern ourselves.

Goethe

It's very important in a leadership role not to place
your ego at the foreground and not to judge everything
in relationship to how your ego is fed.

Ruth J. Simmons

A leader...is like a shepherd. He stays behind the flock,
letting the most nimble go out ahead, whereupon
the others follow, not realizing that all along
they are being directed from behind.

Nelson Mandela

Everyone has an invisible sign hanging from
their neck saying: "Make me feel important!"
Never forget this message when working with people.

Mary Kay Ash

First be the best and then be first.

Grant Tinker

THE SUMMIT OF HAPPINESS
IS REACHED WHEN A PERSON
IS READY TO BE WHAT HE IS.

Erasmus

The man who can make hard things easy is the educator.

Ralph Waldo Emerson

Your time is limited, so don't waste it
living someone else's life.

Steve Jobs

Your purpose will be clear only
when you listen to your heart.

Lolly Daskal

Face the facts of being what you are,
for that is what changes what you are.

Søren Kierkegaard

Our goal should be to live life in radical amazement.... get up in the morning and look at the world in a way that takes nothing for granted. Everything is phenomenal; everything is incredible; never treat life casually.

Abraham Joshua Heschel

Talent hits a target no one else can hit;
Genius hits a target no one else can see.

Arthur Schopenhauer

If you are not willing to risk the unusual,
you will have to settle for the ordinary.

Jim Rohn

Share our similarities, celebrate our differences.

M. Scott Peck

Knowing others is intelligence,
knowing yourself is true wisdom.

Lao Tzu

From each according to his ability,
to each according to his needs.

Karl Marx

No one can predict to what heights you can soar.
Even you will not know until you spread your wings.

Anonymous

Pour yourself into your purpose,
then pour yourself into service.

Lolly Daskal

ACKNOWLEDGMENTS

Alone we can do so little,
together we can do so much.

Lolly Daskal

I want to thank my children, Michaela, Ariel, and Zoe,
for being at the heart of my inspiration and motivation.

I want to also thank Donna Spencer for her endless
dedication and brilliance. I want to thank Frank Sonnenberg
for teaching me what a true supportive friend is, and I want
to thank Carrie Ralston for her artistry and creativity.

And last but not least, I want to thank all my clients who
on a daily basis work toward being the best leaders they
can be by leading from within.

ABOUT LOLLY

Lolly Daskal is a global leadership coach and business consultant who is dedicated to helping cultivate the right values, vision, and culture for individuals and organizations. She is the president and founder of Lead From Within, a global consultancy whose clients include heads of state and CEOs of large multinational companies.

Lolly's coaching, consulting, and speaking use a heart-based leadership approach designed to help people achieve their full potential to make a difference in the world. The *Huffington Post* named Lolly one of its "Most Inspiring Women in the World" and *Inc.* has named Lolly among its "100 Great Leadership Speakers for Your Next Conference."

As the pioneer of heart-based leadership, she is a regular columnist for *Inc.*, *Fast Company*, *Harvard Business Review*, the *Huffington Post*, and *Psychology Today*. Lolly Daskal is one of the most prominent leadership voices of our time.

You can visit Lolly's website and blog or follow her on Twitter and LinkedIn.

Website: lollydaskal.com
Twitter: twitter.com/lollydaskal
LinkedIn: linkedin.com/in/lollydaskal

DID YOU LIKE
THIS BOOK?

Before you go, I'd like to say THANKS for purchasing my book. I know you could have picked from hundreds of leadership books, but you took a chance with me.

A tremendous amount of effort was put into this book to deliver outstanding value and content for you, so please let your own voice be heard in the comments section of our Amazon product page.

If you enjoyed this book it would help us a lot if you would leave an honest review on Amazon. Knowing that you found the book useful will inspire others to find the answers to the heart of their leadership.

Could you please take just a minute to leave a review on Amazon? One sentence is all it takes. Click here to leave a quick review on Amazon. Reviews are the single biggest gift you can give to authors. They are tough to get and count for so much. Thank you!

Made in the USA
Middletown, DE
30 November 2016